The Tastiest Dishes Ever

The Classic Fish Recipe Cookbook That Will Stay for Years to Come

BY: Valeria Ray

License Notes

Copyright © 2019 Valeria Ray All Rights Reserved

All rights to the content of this book are reserved by the Author without exception unless permission is given stating otherwise.

The Author have no claims as to the authenticity of the content and the Reader bears all responsibility and risk when following the content. The Author is not liable for any reparations, damages, accidents, injuries or other incidents occurring from the Reader following all or part of this publication.

A Special Reward for Purchasing My Book!

Thank you, cherished reader, for purchasing my book and taking the time to read it. As a special reward for your decision, I would like to offer a gift of free and discounted books directly to your inbox. All you need to do is fill in the box below with your email address and name to start getting amazing offers in the comfort of your own home. You will never miss an offer because a reminder will be sent to you. Never miss a deal and get great deals without having to leave the house! Subscribe now and start saving!

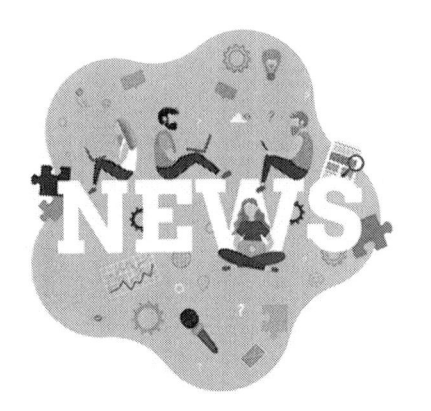

https://valeria-ray.gr8.com

Contents

Classic Fish Recipes 6

(1) Ginger and Sesame Salmon Salad 7

(2) Baked Swordfish Steaks 11

(3) Black Bass with Rosemary Vinaigrette 14

(4) Grilled Halibut 17

(5) Skillet Butter Cod 19

(6) Buffalo Ranch Salmon 22

(7) Baked Tilapia and Spinach Casserole 25

(8) Ginger and Lemon Cod with Broccoli and Rice 28

(9) Thai Coconut Curry Mahi Mahi 32

(10) Sriracha and Butter Cod with Kale 35

(11) Blackened Catfish 38

(12) Roasted Salmon with a Strawberry Salad 41

(13) Sicilian Salmon with Mushrooms 44

(14) Wild Mackerel with Crushed Potatoes 47

(15) Country Oven Fried Fish 51

(16) Chilean Sea Bass with Spinach Pesto 53

(17) Broiled Sesame Salmon 56

(18) Cilantro and Garlic Shrimp 59

(19) Healthy Fish Tacos 62

(20) Seared Flounder with Spinach 65

(21) Pan Roasted Halibut with Corona Beans 68

(22) Glazed Garlic and Honey Salmon 72

(23) Easy Fish Stew 75

(24) Salmon Burgers 78

(25) Sea Bass with Sweet Salsa 81

About the Author 84

Author's Afterthoughts 86

Classic Fish Recipes

MMMMMMMMMMMMMMMMMMMMMMMMMMMM

(1) Ginger and Sesame Salmon Salad

This is a tasty and simple salad dish you can make whenever you are in a hurry. One bite and you will become hooked.

Yield: 4 servings

Cooking Time: 30 minutes

List of Ingredients:

- 2 Tablespoons of soy sauce
- 1, 1 inch piece of ginger, chopped
- 1 clove of garlic, chopped
- 2 Tablespoons of green onions, extra for garnish
- 1 tablespoon of toasted sesame seeds
- ¼ cup of vegetable oil
- 3 Tablespoons of white vinegar
- 2 Tablespoons of honey
- 1 tablespoon of sesame oil, extra for drizzling
- 4 wonton wrappers, cut into thin strips
- Dash of salt and black pepper
- 2 pounds of salmon, cut into 4 fillets
- 1 tablespoon of extra virgin olive oil
- 10 ounces of mixed greens, washed
- 1 cup of carrots, shredded

MMMMMMMMMMMMMMMMMMMMMMMMMMMMMM

Methods:

1. Heat the oven to 475 degrees.
2. In a food processor, add in the soy sauce, chopped ginger, chopped garlic, sliced green onions, toasted sesame seeds, vegetable oil, vinegar, honey and sesame oil. Pulse on the highest setting until smooth in consistency. Set aside in the fridge to chill until ready for use.
3. In a baking sheet. Add the strips of wonton. Drizzle the sesame oil over the top. Season with a dash of salt and black pepper. Toss well to mix. Spread in an even layer. Place into the oven to bake for 5 minutes or until gold.
4. Season the salmon fillets with a dash of salt and black pepper.
5. Place a skillet over high heat. Add in the olive oil. Once the oil begins to smoke, add in the salmon fillets with the skin side facing up. Cook for 4 minutes. Flip and continue to cook for an additional 4 minutes.

6. In a bowl, add in the mixed greens and ginger dressing mix. Toss well until coated.
7. Serve the salmon fillets on a bed of the mixed greens. Garnish with the green onions and drizzle the remaining dressing over the top.

(2) Baked Swordfish Steaks

This is a delicious fish dish you can make if you want to impress your friends and family during special occasions.

Yield: 4 servings

Cooking Time: 20 minutes

List of Ingredients:

- 3 Tablespoons of extra virgin olive oil, evenly divided
- 3 swordfish steaks
- Dash of salt and black pepper
- 2 pints of cherry tomatoes, cut into halves
- ¼ cup of red onion, chopped
- 3 Tablespoons of basil, sliced
- ½ of a lemon, juice only

MMMMMMMMMMMMMMMMMMMMMMMMMMMMM

Methods:

1. Preheat the oven to 400 degrees.
2. In a cast iron skillet set over medium to high heat, add in 2 tablespoons of olive oil. Add in the swordfish steaks. Season with a dash of salt and black pepper. Cook for 3 minutes on each side.
3. Transfer the skillet into the oven. Roast for 10 minutes or until flaky.
4. Prepare the salad. In a bowl, add in the cherry tomato halves, chopped red onion and sliced basil. Add in the 1 tablespoon of olive oil and lemon juice. Season with a dash of salt and black pepper. Stir well to mix.
5. Spoon the salad over the top of the swordfish steaks. Serve.

(3) Black Bass with Rosemary Vinaigrette

This is a fresh tasting fish dish that is perfect to make whenever you have a need to spoil yourself. For a complete meal, be sure to serve this dish with roasted potatoes or a salad.

Yield: 4 servings

Cooking Time: 15 minutes

List of Ingredients:

- 2 Tablespoons of extra virgin olive oil
- 4, 4 ounce black bass fillets, skin scored
- Dash of salt and black pepper
- 2 cloves of garlic, thinly sliced
- 3 Tablespoons of black oil cured olives, pits removed and chopped
- 1 tablespoon of rosemary leaves
- ½ cup of orange juice
- 1 head of radicchio, leaves torn

MMMMMMMMMMMMMMMMMMMMMMMMMMMMMM

Methods:

1. In a skillet set over medium to high heat, add in the olive oil.
2. Season the black bass fillets with a dash of salt and black pepper. Add into the skillet with the skin side facing down. Cook for 5 minutes or until the skin is crispy. Turn the fillets over.
3. Add in the sliced garlic, chopped olives and rosemary leaves. Stir well to mix. Continue to cook for 3 minutes or until the fillets are opaque.
4. Add in the orange juice and swirl around to coat the bottom of the skillet. Remove from heat.
5. Serve the bass fillets with a topping of radicchio and the vinaigrette poured over the top.

(4) Grilled Halibut

This is an easy and delicious fish recipe that is packed with a honey and lemon flavor I know nobody will be able to resist.

Yield: 4 servings

Cooking Time: 15 minutes

List of Ingredients:

- 2 Tablespoons of butter, melted
- 2 Tablespoons of honey
- ½ of a lemon, juice only
- 2 teaspoons of soy sauce
- ½ teaspoons of black pepper
- 2 cloves of garlic, minced
- 1 pound of halibut fillets

MMMMMMMMMMMMMMMMMMMMMMMMMMMMMM

Methods:

1. In a bowl, add in the honey, melted butter, lemon juice, soy sauce and minced garlic. Season with a dash of black pepper. Whisk until smooth in consistency.
2. In a skillet set over medium heat, add in 1 teaspoon of olive oil.
3. Brush the halibut fillets with the sauce mix. Transfer into the skillet. Cook for 2 minutes on each side. Lower the heat to medium. Continue to cook for an additional 2 to 3 minutes or until the fillets flake with a fork.
4. Remove and serve immediately.

(5) Skillet Butter Cod

This is a delicious fish recipe that I am sure will become a family favorite. Even the pickiest of children will love this dish.

Yield: 2 to 4 servings

Cooking Time: 10 minutes

Ingredients for the cod:

- 1 ½ pounds of cod fillets
- 6 Tablespoons of butter, thinly sliced

Ingredients for the seasoning:

- ¼ teaspoons of powdered garlic
- ½ teaspoons of salt
- ¼ teaspoons of black pepper
- ¾ teaspoons of smoked paprika
- Lemon slices, juice only
- Parsley, chopped and for garnish

MMMMMMMMMMMMMMMMMMMMMMMMMMMMMM

Methods:

1. In a bowl, add in the chopped parsley, powdered garlic, dash of salt, smoked paprika and dash of black pepper. Stir well to mix.
2. Season both sides of the cod fillets with the seasoning mix.
3. In a skillet set over medium to high heat, add in 2 tablespoons of butter. Once melted, add in the cod fillets. Cook for 2 minutes.
4. Lower the heat to medium. Flip the cod and top off with the remaining butter. Continue to cook for an additional 3 to 4 minutes or until the cod begins to flake.
5. Drizzle lemon juice from the lemon slices over the fillets.
6. Remove from heat and serve immediately.

(6) Buffalo Ranch Salmon

This is a delicious fish dish that is packed with a spicy flavor you won't be able to get enough of. Those who can't handle a bit of spice should avoid this salmon dish.

Yield: 4 servings

Cooking Time: 25 minutes

List of Ingredients:

- 3 Tablespoons of buffalo hot sauce
- 4 Tablespoons of butter, melted
- 1/3 cup of panko breadcrumbs
- 1 tablespoon of extra virgin olive oil
- 1 tablespoon of Ranch seasoning
- 4, 6 ounce salmon fillets
- Dash of salt and black pepper

MMMMMMMMMMMMMMMMMMMMMMMMMMMMMM

Methods:

1. Preheat the oven to 425 degrees. Grease a baking dish with cooking spray.
2. In a bowl, add in the melted butter and buffalo hot sauce. Whisk well to mix.
3. In a separate bowl, add in the panko breadcrumbs, olive oil and ranch seasoning. Stir well to mix.
4. Place the salmon fillets onto the baking sheet with the skin side facing down. Pour the buffalo sauce mix over each fillet. Sprinkle the panko breadcrumb mix over the top. Press down.
5. Place the fillets into the oven to bake for 15 minutes or until the salmon is cooked through.
6. Remove and serve immediately.

(7) Baked Tilapia and Spinach Casserole

This is the perfect casserole dish you can make whenever you need to feed a large group of people. This tilapia dish is smothered in a creamy sauce that you won't be able to resist.

Yield: 8 servings

Cooking Time: 10 minutes

List of Ingredients:

- 1 pound of tilapia fillets
- 1, 8 ounce bag of spinach
- 3 Tablespoons of butter, thinly sliced
- 1 cup of Monterey jack cheese, shredded

Ingredients for the sauce:

- ½ cup of mayonnaise
- ½ cup of sour cream
- ½ cups of grated Parmesan cheese
- 2 cloves of garlic, crushed
- 1 teaspoon of old bay seasoning
- ½ teaspoons of adobo seasoning
- ¼ teaspoons of black pepper
- Dash of salt

MMMMMMMMMMMMMMMMMMMMMMMMMMMMMM

Methods:

1. In a baking dish, add the spinach. Top off with the sliced butter.
2. Add a layer of the tilapia fillets over the top.
3. Prepare the sauce. In a bowl, add in the mayonnaise, sour cream, grated Parmesan cheese, crushed garlic, old bay seasoning, adobo, black pepper and dash of salt. Stir well to mix. Spread over the top of the tilapia fillets.
4. Sprinkle the shredded Monterey jack cheese over the top.
5. Place into the oven to bake for 10 minutes at 500 degrees.
6. Remove and serve immediately.

(8) Ginger and Lemon Cod with Broccoli and Rice

This is a fish dish that you will soon become addicted to. It is a simple fish dish made with a tangy flavor you won't be able to get enough of.

Yield: 4 servings

Cooking Time: 25 minutes

List of Ingredients:

- 1 pound of broccoli florets
- Extra virgin olive oil, as needed
- Dash of salt and black pepper
- 1 pack of rice pilaf
- 1 tablespoon of ginger, grated
- 1 clove of garlic, grated
- 2 lemons, cut into wheels
- 1 pounds of cod, divided into 3 inch sized pieces
- ½ cup of dried white wine
- ¼ cup of parsley, chopped

MMMMMMMMMMMMMMMMMMMMMMMMMMMMMMM

Methods:

1. Preheat the oven to 450 degrees. Place a sheet of parchment paper onto a baking sheet.
2. Place the broccoli florets onto the baking sheet. Drizzle 1 tablespoon of olive oil over the florets. Season with a dash of salt and black pepper. Toss well to mix.
3. Place into the oven to bake for 20 minutes or until golden.
4. Prepare the rice pilaf according to the directions on the package.
5. In a bowl, add in 1 tablespoon of olive oil, grated ginger, grated garlic, lemon wheels and a dash of salt. Stir well to mix.
6. Place a skillet over medium to high heat. Add in 2 tablespoons of olive oil. Once the oil begins to smoke, season the cod pieces with a dash of salt. Add into the skillet and sear for 5 minutes. Move to one side of the skillet. Add the ginger and lemon mix to the free side of the skillet. Cook for 3 minutes.

7. Add in the dried white wine and chopped parsley. Continue to cook for 3 minutes. Pour the sauce over the cod fillets.
8. Add in the prepare rice pilaf. Continue to cook for 3 minutes. Add in the roasted broccoli florets.
9. Remove from heat and serve with a garnish of chopped parsley.

(9) Thai Coconut Curry Mahi Mahi

Make this delicious fish dish whenever you are craving something on the exotic side. Serve with basmati rice for the tastiest results.

Yield: 4 servings

Cooking Time: 40 minutes

List of Ingredients:

- 1, 13.5 ounce can of unsweetened coconut milk
- 1 tablespoon of lime juice
- 1 tablespoon of Thai red curry paste
- 1 teaspoon of white sugar
- 4 teaspoons of ginger, peeled and minced
- 2 cloves of garlic, minced
- 1 teaspoon of fish sauce
- 2 Tablespoons of cilantro, chopped and extra for serving
- 2 Tablespoons of scallions, minced and extra for serving
- 4, 6 ounce mahi mahi fillets

Methods:

1. In a saucepan set over medium heat, add in the coconut milk, lime juice, curry paste, white sugar, minced ginger, minced garlic and fish sauce. Whisk well to mix. Allow to come to a boil. Lower the heat to low and cook for 8 to 10 minutes or until thick in consistency.
2. Remove from heat.
3. Add in the chopped cilantro and minced scallions. Stir well to mix. Set aside to cool slightly.
4. Season with a dash of salt and black pepper. Pour ¼ cup of the sauce aside for marinating. Set the remaining sauce aside for later use.
5. Preheat the oven to 400 degrees. Place a sheet of parchment paper onto a baking sheet.
6. Place the fillets onto the baking sheet. Season with a dash of salt and black pepper. Brush with ¼ cup of the sauce.
7. Place the fillets into the oven to bake for 15 to 20 minutes or until cooked through.
8. Remove and serve immediately with the remaining sauce drizzled over the top. Garnish with extra cilantro and scallions.

(10) Sriracha and Butter Cod with Kale

This cod fillet is smothered in a spicy butter sauce which can add some much-needed spice to a relatively healthy meal.

Yield: 4 servings

Cooking Time: 20 minutes

List of Ingredients:

- 2 Tablespoons of extra virgin olive oil, evenly divided
- 2 cloves of garlic, minced
- Dash of salt and black pepper
- 1 bunch of kale, chopped
- 3 Tablespoons of butter
- 2 teaspoons of sriracha sauce
- ¼ cup of low sodium chicken stock
- 3 green onions, thinly sliced and evenly divided
- 4, 6 to 8 ounce cod fillets

Methods:

1. Preheat the oven to 400 degrees.
2. In a bowl, add in 1 tablespoon of olive oil, minced garlic, dash of salt and black pepper. Whisk until mixed. Add in kale. Toss well to coat. Transfer onto a baking sheet.
3. Place into the oven to bake for 10 to 12 minutes or until crispy.
4. In a saucepan set over medium to high heat, add in the butter. Once melted, add in the Sriracha sauce, chicken stock and dash of salt. Allow to simmer for 5 minutes. Add in half of the green onions. Toss well to mix. Cover and set aside.
5. In a skillet set over medium to high heat, add in 1 tablespoon of olive oil. Season the cod fillets with a dash of salt and black pepper. Add into the skillet. Cook for 2 minutes on each side. Transfer onto a plate and set aside.
6. Serve with the crispy kale and a spoonful of Sriracha sauce. Garnish with the remaining green onions.

(11) Blackened Catfish

This is a delicious New Orleans dish that you will love. Served with a spicy rice, this is a delicious dish that every spicy food lover won't be able to get enough of.

Yield: 2 servings

Cooking Time: 55 minutes

Ingredients for the catfish:

- 2 catfish fillets
- 2 to 3 Tablespoons of old bay seasoning
- 2 Tablespoons of extra virgin olive oil

Ingredients for the Cajun rice:

- 1 cup of brown rice
- 1 ½ cups of water
- 2 Tablespoons of extra virgin olive oil
- 1 to 2 cloves of garlic, minced
- ½ cup of green bell pepper, chopped
- ½ cup of white onion, chopped
- ½ teaspoons of powdered garlic
- 2 teaspoons of Cajun seasoning
- Dash of salt and black pepper

MMMMMMMMMMMMMMMMMMMMMMMMMMMMMMM

Methods:

1. In a saucepan set over medium to high heat, add in 1 ½ cups of water. Allow to come to a boil. Add in the rice and lower the heat to low. Cover and cook for 45 minutes or until cooked. Remove from heat and set aside.
2. Season the catfish fillets with the old bay seasoning until coated on both sides.
3. In a skillet set over medium heat, add in the olive oil. Add in the catfish fillets. Cook for 3 to 4 minutes on each side or until the fillets begin to flake. Transfer onto a plate and set aside.
4. Clean the skillet and add another 2 tablespoons of olive oil. Add in the minced garlic, chopped green bell pepper and chopped onion. Stir well to mix. Cook for 5 to 8 minutes or until soft.
5. Add the vegetables, powdered garlic, Cajun seasoning, dash of salt and black pepper into the rice. Stir well to mix.
6. Serve the catfish fillets with the Cajun rice.

(12) Roasted Salmon with a Strawberry Salad

This is a healthy and delicious lunch whenever you are craving something on the healthy side. You don't have to feel guilty about enjoying it.

Yield: 4 servings

Cooking Time: 30 minutes

List of Ingredients:

- 4 salmon fillets
- ¼ cup of extra virgin olive oil, extra for drizzling
- Dash of salt and black pepper
- 2 lemons, cut into wheels
- 2 Tablespoons of balsamic vinegar
- 1 tablespoon of Dijon mustard
- 16 ounces of strawberries, thinly sliced
- 10 ounces of arugula greens
- ½ of a red onion, thinly sliced
- 2 Tablespoons of chives, chopped

MMMMMMMMMMMMMMMMMMMMMMMMMMMMMM

Methods:

1. Preheat the oven to 450 degrees. Place a sheet of parchment paper onto a baking sheet.
2. Rinse the salmon fillets under running water. Pat dry with a few paper towels. Drizzle olive oil over the fillets. Season with a dash of salt and black pepper. Place onto the baking sheet.
3. Add the lemon wheels over the salmon fillets.
4. Place into the oven to bake for 10 to 12 minutes or until baked through. Remove and set aside to rest.
5. In a bowl, add in the vinegar, Dijon mustard, extra virgin olive oil, dash of salt and black pepper. Whisk until mixed. Add in the arugula greens and sliced onion. Toss well to mix.
6. Divide the salad among serving plates. Top off with the salmon fillets.
7. Serve with a garnish of chopped chives.

(13) Sicilian Salmon with Mushrooms

If you are looking for a healthy and delicious dinner dish to serve any night of the week, then this is the perfect dish for you to make.

Yield: 1 serving

Cooking Time: 1 hour

Ingredients for the fish:

- 3 ½ ounces of salmon fillets, skin removed
- 1 lime, juice only
- Extra virgin olive oil, for drizzling
- ½ teaspoons of dried chili flakes
- 1 teaspoon of smoked paprika
- Dash of salt and black pepper

Ingredients for the mushrooms:

- 1 tablespoon of extra virgin olive oil
- 3 ½ ounces of button mushrooms, thinly sliced
- 3 ½ ounces of broccoli, chopped
- 1 clove of garlic, chopped
- 2 Tablespoons of parsley, chopped

MMMMMMMMMMMMMMMMMMMMMMMMMMMMMMM

Methods:

1. Preheat the oven to 350 degrees.
2. In a baking dish, add in the salmon fillets. Drizzle olive oil over the top. Add in the lime juice, dried chili flakes and smoked paprika. Season with a dash of salt and black pepper.
3. Place into the oven to bake for 10 minutes or until cooked through.
4. In a skillet set over medium heat, add in 1 tablespoon of olive oil. Add in the sliced mushrooms. Cook for 5 minutes. Add in the chopped broccoli and cook for 2 to 3 minutes or until soft.
5. Add in the chopped garlic. Continue to cook for an additional minute.
6. Add in the chopped parsley. Stir well to incorporate. Remove from heat.
7. Serve the mushrooms and broccoli over the top of the salmon fillets.

(14) Wild Mackerel with Crushed Potatoes

This is the perfect fish dish to serve to your significant other whenever you want to surprise them with something special.

Yield: 4 servings

Cooking Time: 50 minutes

List of Ingredients:

- 2 pounds of waxy potatoes
- Dash of salt and black pepper
- 1 cup of plain Greek yogurt
- 1 teaspoon of lemon juice
- 1 teaspoon of white wine vinegar
- 4 cloves of garlic, peeled and crushed
- 5 Tablespoons of extra virgin olive oil, evenly divided
- 4, 6 ounce mackerel fillets, skin-on
- 2 Tablespoons of oregano leaves
- 1 teaspoon of lemon zest, grated
- Dash of sea salt

Methods:

1. In a pot set over high heat, fill with water. Add in the waxy potatoes and season with a dash of salt. Allow to come to a boil. Lower the heat to low and cook for 10 to 12 minutes or until soft. Drain and set the potatoes aside to cool.
2. Preheat the oven to broil.
3. In a bowl, add in the Greek yogurt, lemon juice and white wine vinegar. Whisk to mix. Season with a dash of salt and black pepper. Set aside.
4. Place the potatoes onto a baking sheet. Press with the bottom of a glass to flatten.
5. On the baking sheet, add in the crushed garlic and 4 tablespoons of olive oil. Toss well to coat. Season with a dash of salt and black pepper. Place into the oven to broil for 10 to 12 minutes or until golden.
6. Spread 1 tablespoon of olive oil onto the skin side of the mackerel. Season with a dash of salt and black pepper. Place onto the baking sheet on top of the potatoes with the skin side facing up.
7. Place into the oven to broil for 10 to 12 minutes or until the skin is crispy.
8. Remove. Top off with the oregano leaves and grated lemon zest.

9. Spread the yogurt sauce over serving plates. Top off with the potatoes and mackerel. Sprinkle a dash of sea salt over the top.
10. Serve immediately.

(15) Country Oven Fried Fish

This is a deliciously simple fish dish that you can make any night of the week after work. Since it is made in the oven, you don't have to bother with splashes of oil in your kitchen.

Yield: 4 servings

Cooking Time: 15 minutes

List of Ingredients:

- 1 pound of cod fillets, boneless and skinless
- 4 teaspoons of vegetable oil
- 4 Tablespoons of seasoned breadcrumbs
- 1 tablespoon of lemon juice
- ½ teaspoons of smoked paprika
- Dash of salt and black pepper
- Lemon wedges, for serving

Methods:

1. Preheat the oven to 450 degrees.
2. In a shallow dish, add in the vegetable oil and lemon juice. Stir well to mix. On a plate, add in the seasoned breadcrumbs, dash of salt, black pepper and smoked paprika. Stir well to mix.
3. Dip the cod fillets in the oil mix. Roll in the breadcrumb mixture until coated on both sides. Transfer onto a baking sheet.
4. Place into the oven to bake for 8 to 10 minutes or until golden.
5. Remove and serve immediately with the lemon wedges.

(16) Chilean Sea Bass with Spinach Pesto

This is the perfect dish to make to celebrate a special occasion such as an anniversary or a birthday. It is a dish that can be made in under 30 minutes.

Yield: 4 servings

Cooking Time: 30 minutes

List of Ingredients:

- 2 pounds of wild Chilean sea bass fillets
- Dash of salt and black pepper
- 2 cups of baby spinach
- ½ cup of parsley, chopped and extra for garnish
- 1 clove of garlic, smashed
- ¼ cup of walnuts, chopped
- 2 teaspoons of lemon juice
- Extra virgin olive oil, as needed
- 1 avocado, pit removed
- 1 pound of asparagus, trimmed
- 2 lemons, sliced in half
- Dash of sea salt

MMMMMMMMMMMMMMMMMMMMMMMMMMMMMM

Methods:

1. Season the sea bass fillets with a dash of salt and black pepper.
2. In a bowl of a food processor, add in the baby spinach, smashed garlic, chopped walnuts, lemon juice, ¼ cup of extra virgin olive oil, dash of salt and black pepper. Pulse for 10 seconds. Add in the avocado and pulse well to blend.
3. Place a skillet over high heat. Add in 1 tablespoon of olive oil. Once the oil begins to smoke. Add in the sea bass fillets. Sear on one side for 3 minutes. Transfer onto a plate and set aside.
4. Set the skillet back over medium to high heat. Add in 1 teaspoon of olive oil, asparagus and dash of salt. Cook for 5 minutes or until soft. Transfer onto a serving plate.
5. Add the lemons into the skillet with the cut side facing down. Sear for 1 minute. Transfer onto the plate with the asparagus.
6. Place the sea bass over the asparagus.
7. Pour the pesto over the top.
8. Serve with a garnish of parsley and sea salt.

(17) Broiled Sesame Salmon

This is a dish you can serve during your next dinner event. It makes for a sizzling dish that will impress your dinner guests.

Yield: 3 servings

Cooking Time: 45 minutes

List of Ingredients:

- 2 cloves of garlic, thinly sliced
- 3 Tablespoons of lime juice
- 2 Tablespoons of soy sauce
- 2 teaspoons of honey
- 1 tablespoon + 2 teaspoons of vegetable oil
- ½ teaspoons of sesame seeds, extra for serving
- 3, 8 ounce salmon fillets, skin on and center cut
- Dash of salt
- 1 bunch of scallions
- 1 Fresno chile, thinly sliced

MMMMMMMMMMMMMMMMMMMMMMMMMMMMMMM

Methods:

1. In a bowl, add in the sliced garlic, lime juice, soy sauce, honey, 1 tablespoon of vegetable oil and the sesame seeds. Whisk well until mixed.
2. Season the salmon fillets with a dash of salt. Transfer into a Ziploc bag. Pour in half of the marinade and seal the bag. Set aside to marinate for 30 minutes. Set the remaining marinade aside for later use.
3. Preheat the oven to broil.
4. In a bowl, add in the bunch of scallions and 2 teaspoons of vegetable oil. Toss to coat. Transfer onto a baking sheet. Place into the oven to broil for 3 minutes.
5. Remove the salmon fillets from the marinade. Place on top of the scallions. Pour some of the reserved marinade over the top. Place back into the oven to broil for 6 minutes or until the edges are charred.
6. Pour more of the reserved marinade over the fillets. Top off with the sliced chile. Continue to broil for 2 minutes.
7. Remove and serve with a garnish of sesame seeds.

(18) Cilantro and Garlic Shrimp

Dinner has never been easier with the help of this delicious dish. It is perfect to make for those fish lovers in your home.

Yield: 2 to 4 servings

Cooking Time: 20 minutes

List of Ingredients:

- 4 Tablespoons of extra virgin olive oil, evenly divided
- 3 cloves of garlic, minced
- 2 teaspoons of lime juice
- ½ teaspoons of powdered chili
- ¼ teaspoons of salt
- 1/3 cup of cilantro, chopped and extra for serving
- 1 pound of shrimp, peeled and deveined
- 1/3 cup of onion, chopped

MMMMMMMMMMMMMMMMMMMMMMMMMMMMMMM

Methods:

1. In a bowl, add in 3 tablespoons of olive oil, minced garlic, lime juice, powdered chili, dash of salt and chopped cilantro. Stir well to mix. Add in the shrimp and toss well to coat.
2. Cover and set into the fridge to chill for 10 minutes.
3. In a skillet set over medium to high heat, add in 1 tablespoon of olive oil. Add in the onions. Cook for 3 to 5 minutes or until soft.
4. Add in the shrimp mix and cook for 1 minute on each side or until bright pink and cooked through.
5. Remove. Serve immediately with the chopped cilantro.

(19) Healthy Fish Tacos

This is a delicious fish recipe I know you will want to make as often as possible. Feel free to top off with your favorite toppings.

Yield: 4 servings

Cooking Time: 35 minutes

List of Ingredients:

- ¼ cup of low-fat sour cream
- 2 Tablespoons of lime juice
- Dash of salt and black pepper
- 1 jalapeno pepper, cut into halves
- 2 ½ cups of red cabbage, shredded
- 4 green onions, thinly sliced
- 2 Tablespoons of extra virgin olive oil
- 1 pound of tilapia fillets, sliced into strips
- 8, 6 inch flour tortillas
- ½ cup of cilantro, chopped

MMMMMMMMMMMMMMMMMMMMMMMMMMMMMM

Methods:

1. In a bowl, add in the sour cream and lime juice. Stir well to mix. Season with a dash of salt and black pepper.
2. In a separate bowl, add in the shredded red cabbage, sliced green onions and minced jalapeno pepper halves. Add in half of the sour cream mix. Toss well until coated.
3. In a skillet set over medium heat, add in the olive oil. Season the tilapia fillet strips with a dash of salt and black pepper. Add into the skillet along with half of the jalapeno mix. Cook for 5 minutes on each side or until golden. Toss the jalapeno mix out.
4. Add the fish strips onto the tortillas. Top off with the slaw, chopped cilantro and sour cream.
5. Serve immediately.

(20) Seared Flounder with Spinach

While the spinach is delicious all on its own, with the seared flounder, it helps to tur a boring healthy meal into a flavorful one.

Yield: 4 servings

Cooking Time: 20 minutes

List of Ingredients:

- 2 Tablespoons of vegetable oil, evenly divided
- 1 clove of garlic, chopped
- 1 teaspoon of ginger, peeled and grated
- 1 bunch of flat leaf spinach, trimmed and chopped
- 1 tablespoon of toasted sesame oil
- 1 tablespoon of rice vinegar
- 2 teaspoons of low sodium soy sauce
- 2 teaspoons of toasted sesame seeds
- Dash of salt and black pepper
- 4, 6 ounce flounder fillets

MMMMMMMMMMMMMMMMMMMMMMMMMMMMMM

Methods:

1. In a skillet set over medium to high heat, add in 1 tablespoon of vegetable oil. Add in the chopped garlic and grated ginger. Stir well to mix. Cook for 2 minutes or until fragrant.
2. Add in the chopped spinach and sesame oil. Toss well to coat. Continue to cook for 5 minutes or until the spinach is wilted.
3. Add in the rice vinegar, soy sauce and toasted sesame seeds. Season with a dash of salt and black pepper. Toss well to mix. Remove and set aside.
4. In a separate skillet set over medium to high heat, add in 1 tablespoon of vegetable oil. Season the flounder fillets with a dash of salt and black pepper. Cook for 3 minutes on each side or until gold. Remove and transfer onto a serving plate.
5. Serve the flounder with the spinach.

(21) Pan Roasted Halibut with Corona Beans

This halibut dish is made by bring the cod fillets in salt water, which help to give it a naturally salty flavor that makes it even more delicious.

Yield: 6 servings

Cooking Time: 2 hours and 50 minutes

List of Ingredients:

- 1 ½ cups of corona beans, soaked overnight
- 1 shallot, sliced into halves
- 2 bay leaves, sliced in half
- 1 ½ Tablespoons + ¼ cup of salt, extra if needed
- 2 anchovy fillets, drained and chopped
- 1 clove of garlic, grated
- ¾ cup of parsley, chopped
- 1 tablespoon of capers, drained and chopped
- 1 tablespoon of lemon zest, grated
- 1 tablespoon of lemon juice
- ½ cup + 1 tablespoon of olive oil
- Dash of black pepper
- 6, 5 ounce halibut fillets, skinless
- 1 tablespoon of butter, soft
- 1 lemon, sliced into wedges

MMMMMMMMMMMMMMMMMMMMMMMMMMMMMMM

Methods:

1. Drain the beans from the soaking water and transfer into a pot. Cover by 2 inches with water. Add in the shallot halves, bay leaves and 1 ½ tablespoon of salt. Set over high heat and allow to come to a boil. Lower the heat to low. Cook for 1 ½ to 2 hours or until the beans are soft. Remove and set aside to cool completely.
2. In a bowl, add in the anchovies, grated garlic, capers, chopped parsley, fresh lemon zest, lemon juice and ½ cup of olive oil. Season with a dash of salt and black pepper. Stir well to mix
3. Drain the beans. Toss out the shallots and bay leaves. Transfer into the parsley mix. Toss well to coat. Season with a dash of salt and lemon juice.
4. In a baking dish, add in ¼ cup of salt and 4 cups of water. Stir well until dissolved. Add in the halibut fillets. Set aside to rest for 30 minutes. Remove and pat dry with a few paper towels.
5. In a skillet set over medium to high heat, add in 1 tablespoon of olive oil. Add in the halibut fillets. Cook for 4 minutes or until golden. Flip and continue to cook for an additional minute. Remove from heat.

6. Add the butter into the skillet. Allow to rest for 1 minute.
7. Serve the halibut fillets with the beans and a garnish of lemon wedges.

(22) Glazed Garlic and Honey Salmon

This is a delicious salmon dish you can make whenever you are craving something on the sweeter side. It is so tasty, I know you will want to make it as often as possible.

Yield: 4 servings

Cooking Time: 20 minutes

List of Ingredients:

- 1/3 cup of honey
- ¼ cup of soy sauce
- 2 Tablespoons of lemon juice
- 1 teaspoon of crushed red pepper flakes
- 3 Tablespoons of extra virgin olive oil, evenly divided
- 4, 6 ounce salmon fillets, dried
- Dash of salt and black pepper
- 3 cloves of garlic, minced
- 1 lemon, sliced into rounds
- Parsley, chopped and for garnish

MMMMMMMMMMMMMMMMMMMMMMMMMMMMMMM

Methods:

1. In a bowl, add in the honey, soy sauce, lemon juice and crushed red pepper flakes. Whisk well until mixed.
2. In a skillet set over medium to high heat, add in the 2 tablespoons of olive oil. Add in the salmon with the skin side facing up. Season with a dash of salt and black pepper. Cook for 6 minutes or until gold. Flip and add in 1 tablespoon of olive oil.
3. Add in the minced garlic. Cook for 1 minute.
4. Pour in the honey mix and sliced lemon rounds. Continue to cook for 3 to 5 minutes or until reduced. Baste the salmon.
5. Remove from heat. Serve with a garnish of lemon and chopped parsley.

(23) Easy Fish Stew

This is the ultimate stew dish you can make whenever you need something warm and filling to enjoy during the winter.

Yield: 4 servings

Cooking Time: 30 minutes

List of Ingredients:

- 6 Tablespoons of extra virgin olive oil
- 1 onion, chopped
- 3 cloves of garlic, minced
- 2/3 cup of parsley, chopped
- 1 ½ cups of tomato, chopped
- 2 teaspoons of tomato paste
- 8 ounces of clam juice
- ½ cup of dried white wine
- 1 ½ pound of halibut fillets, cut into pieces
- Dash of dried oregano
- Dash of dried thyme
- 1/8 teaspoons of Tabasco sauce
- Dash of salt and black pepper

MMMMMMMMMMMMMMMMMMMMMMMMMMMMMMM

Methods:

1. In a pot set over medium to high heat, add in the olive oil. Add in the onion. Cook for 5 minutes or until soft.
2. Add in the minced garlic. Cook for an additional minute.
3. Add in the chopped parsley. Cook for 2 minutes. Add in the tomato paste and chopped tomato. Stir well to mix. Cook for 10 minutes.
4. Add in the clam juice, dried white wine and halibut fillet pieces. Allow to come to a simmer. Cook for 5 minutes or until the halibut fillets are cooked through.
5. Add in the dried oregano, dried thyme and Tabasco sauce. Season with a dash of salt and black pepper. Stir well to mix.
6. Remove and serve immediately.

(24) Salmon Burgers

This is a healthy and light dinner you can make whenever you need something simple and easy to prepare for your family.

Yield: 3 servings

Cooking Time: 20 minutes

List of Ingredients:

- 1, 14 ounce can of salmon, drained
- 1 egg, beaten
- ½ cup of breadcrumbs
- 1 clove of garlic, minced
- 1 lemon, zest and juice only
- 2 Tablespoons of dill, minced
- 1 tablespoon of Dijon mustard
- 1 teaspoon of Worcestershire sauce
- ½ teaspoons of crushed red pepper flakes
- Dash of salt and black pepper
- 1 tablespoon of extra virgin olive oil
- Hamburger buns, for serving
- Mayonnaise, for serving
- Romaine lettuce, for serving
- Tomato slices, for serving
- Red onion slices, for serving

MMMMMMMMMMMMMMMMMMMMMMMMMMMMMMM

Methods:

1. In a bowl, add in the drained salmons, breadcrumbs, beaten egg, minced garlic, lemon zest, minced dill, Dijon mustard, Worcestershire sauce, crushed red pepper flakes and lemon juice. Stir well to mix.
2. Season with a dash of salt and black pepper.
3. Shape the mix into 4 patties.
4. In a skillet set over medium heat, add in the olive oil. Add in the salmon patties. Cook for 5 minutes on each side or until golden.
5. Transfer the patties onto the buns.
6. Top off with the mayonnaise, romaine lettuce, tomato slices and red onion slices.
7. Serve.

(25) Sea Bass with Sweet Salsa

If you need an elegant fish dish to serve during those special occasion, then this is the perfect seafood dish for you to prepare.

Yield: 4 servings

Cooking Time: 15 minutes

List of Ingredients:

- 2 ½ Tablespoons of extra virgin olive oil, evenly divided
- ¾ teaspoons of salt, evenly divided
- ¾ teaspoons of black pepper, evenly divided
- ½ teaspoons of smoked paprika
- 4, 6 ounce sea bass fillets, skinless
- 1 pink grapefruit, peeled and cut into wedges
- 1 navel orange, peeled and cut into wedges
- 3 Tablespoons of cilantro, chopped
- 1 tablespoon of lime juice
- 1 teaspoon of garlic, minced
- ¼ cup of white onion, thinly sliced

MMMMMMMMMMMMMMMMMMMMMMMMMMMMMM

Methods:

1. Preheat the oven to a high broil.
2. In a bowl, add in 1 ½ teaspoons of olive oil, smoked paprika, dash of black pepper and salt. Stir well to mix. Rub the sea bass fillets with the oil mix. Place onto a baking sheet.
3. Place into the oven to broil for 10 to 12 minutes or until the bass begins to flake. Remove and set aside to rest.
4. In a separate bowl, add in the chopped cilantro, lime juice, minced garlic and 2 tablespoons of olive oil. Season with a dash of salt and black pepper. Add in the sliced white onion, grapefruit wedges and navel orange wedges. Stir well to mix.
5. Spoon the salsa over the sea bass fillets.
6. Serve immediately.

About the Author

A native of Indianapolis, Indiana, Valeria Ray found her passion for cooking while she was studying English Literature at Oakland City University. She decided to try a cooking course with her friends and the experience changed her forever. She enrolled at the Art Institute of Indiana which offered extensive courses in the culinary Arts. Once Ray dipped her toe in the cooking world, she never looked back.

When Valeria graduated, she worked in French restaurants in the Indianapolis area until she became the head chef at one of the 5-star establishments in the area. Valeria's attention to taste and visual detail caught the eye of a local business person who expressed an interest in publishing her recipes. Valeria began her secondary career authoring cookbooks and e-books which she tackled with as much talent and gusto as her first career. Her passion for food leaps off the page of her books which have colourful anecdotes and stunning pictures of dishes she has prepared herself.

Valeria Ray lives in Indianapolis with her husband of 15 years, Tom, her daughter, Isobel and their loveable Golden Retriever, Goldy. Valeria enjoys cooking special dishes in her large, comfortable kitchen where the family gets involved in preparing meals. This successful, dynamic chef is an inspiration to culinary students and novice cooks everywhere.

Author's Afterthoughts

Thank you for Purchasing my book and taking the time to read it from front to back. I am always grateful when a reader chooses my work and I hope you enjoyed it!

With the vast selection available online, I am touched that you chose to be purchasing my work and take valuable time out of your life to read it. My hope is that you feel you made the right decision.

I very much would like to know what you thought of the book. Please take the time to write an honest and informative review on Amazon.com. Your experience and opinions will be of great benefit to me and those readers looking to make an informed choice.

With much thanks,

Valeria Ray